The Crochet Royal Family

BY BEPO & PIGLET CROCHET CREATIONS

Other crochet books available from
Bepo and Piglet Crochet Creations

Birthing Buddies from Antarctica

Halloween Quick Crochet Characters

Birthing Buddies from Africa

This book is dedicated to my family, friends and loyal customers.
Without all your support this book, previous books I've written and future books to come wouldn't exist!

Thank you for believing in me and supporting my dreams. I can never thankyou enough!

Introduction

A lovely customer set me the challenge to make her a crochet HRH The Queen.

I love a challenge, so I jumped at the chance...this book spiraled from making The Queen, into the whole family, including The Queen at the very start of her 70-year reign in 1952 at her coronation.

Materials, tools and stitches

The materials used throughout this book are detailed below.

I use double-knit wool, sometimes called light worsted or 8ply, depending where in the world you are. It really does not matter if you choose to use acrylic, cotton or thicker or thinner types of wool throughout, just keep in mind these may change the size of your finished project.

My favorite 'go to' crochet hook is a 2.25mm, metric size. (UK-13, US-B/11), when I use the double-knit wool. I find the smaller hook keeps my stitches nice and neat.

Again, choose your hook to suit you and the type of wool you choose to use.

The colour wools I used in this book can be substituted for colours of your preference.

I do not stick to one brand but tend to shop around and select colours that jump out at me or are most suitable.

Throughout I have used 9mm safety eyes throughout. The eyes can be embroidered on if you prefer, using a small amount of white or colour coordinated wool.

The fiber fill I use...does not have to cost a fortune. I buy a large cushion inner from a local high street store and use the stuffing in the pillow. Over the years I have saved so much money by using these.
All of these are items are available through online stores.

Accessories used can be found online or any large craft stores. I found the following items when visiting local stores.

Stitches

Stitches used in this book are shown below.

Let us start with the magic ring. [Mr]

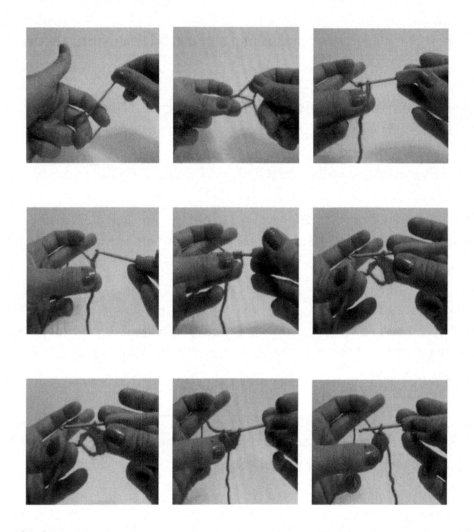

Make a slip knot.
Insert the hook through the center of the circle and pull up a loop of yarn, this will make a chain stitch that will secure your circle.

Yarn over and place hook through the center of the circle, pulling up another loop. You will now have three loops on your hook, yarn through all the loops on your hook and you have completed one stitch.

Repeat for the number of stitches required in your magic circle.

Pull the long tail to tighten the magic circle and slip stitch into the first stich you made.

You have now completed your magic ring and can advance onto the next round.

Throughout he patterns in this book, I use the same stitch, this stitch I find gives structure but works up into a nice soft character.

In the UK, this stitch is called a DOUBLE CROCHET (DC)
In the US, this stitch is called a SINGLE CROCHET (SC)
Yarn over and place hook through your stitch.
Pull up a loop through the stitch and pull through the one your hook.

Puffball stitch.
Make 1 stitch, then repeat four more times, you will have five loops on your hook. On the sixth stitch take the wool through all loops on the hook and continue per pattern.

(DEC)
When asked to decrease in a pattern, you join the next two stiches together to reduce the number of stitches in each row.

(INC)
When asked to increase in a pattern, you make two stitches in the stitch, Increasing the row count.

Parentheses and brackets

An explanation of how the patterns is written is detailed below,
For example, when written

(3, Dec) X 2, 3, (Inc, 3) X 2 (19)

(Make 1 stitch in the next 3 stitches, then decrease) do this twice (X2),
Make 1 stitch in the next 3 stitches, (Increase in the next stitch, make 1
stitch in the next 3 stitches) do this twice (X2). (The total number of
stitches in this round or row)

Let's begin...

Coronation Queen 1952

Coronation Queen 1952

<u>Head – In flesh colour</u>

1. 6mr

2. (inc) x6 (12)

3. (1, inc) x6 (18)

4. (2, inc) x6 (24)

5. (3, inc) x6 (30)

6. (4, inc) x6 (36)

7. (5, inc) x6 (42)

8. (6, inc) x6 (48)

9 – 12. Make 1 stitch in each (48)

13. Make 1 in the next 24 stitches, make puffball stitch x1, make 1 in the remaining 23 stitches (48)

14 – 15. Make 1 in each stitch (48)

16. (6, dec) x6 (42)

17. (5, dec) x6 (36)

18. (4, dec) x6 (30)

19. (3, dec) x6 (24)

20. (2, dec) x6 (18)

21. (1, dec) x6 (12)

Insert eyes at row 11 with five stitches in-between and stuff the head.

22-23. Make 1 in each (12)

24.(1, inc) x1, make 1 in the next 3, (inc) x1, make 1 in the remaining 6 stitches (14)

25. Make 1 in the next 3 stitches, (inc) x2, Make 1 in the next 7 stitches, (inc) x2 (18)

26. Make 1 in each stitch (18).

Finish off flesh colour.

Dress – In white.

Join at the previous finish off point.

1. Make 1 in each (18)

2. (8, inc) x1, (inc, 2) x1, (inc) x2, Make 1 in the remaining 4 stitches. (22)

3. Make 1 in the next 1o stitches, *(inc) x2, make 1 in the next 2 stitches, (inc) x2, make 1 in the remaining 6 stitches (26)

4-5. Make 1 in each (26)

6. Make 1 in the next 11 stitches, (dec) x5, make 1 in the remaining 7 stitches (23)

7. (6, dec) x1, (8, dec) x1, make 1 in the remaining 3 stitches (19)

8-9. Make 1 in each (19)

10. (1, inc) x9 (28)

11. (2, inc) x9, Make 1 in remaining stitch (37)

12. Make 1 in each (37)

13. (5, inc) x7, Make 1 in remaining stitch (43)

14-24. Make 1 in each (43)

25. Turn your work so the opposite side of your work is facing you, Make 1 front post crochet around (43)

26.Turn your work to face the way you were previously working, (5, dec) x7, make 1 in the last stitch (37)

27. (4, dec) x6, make 1 in the remaining stitch (31)

Stuff the skirt area.

28. (3, dec) x6, make 1 in remaining stitch (25)

29. (2, dec) x6, make 1 in the remaining stitch (19)

30. (dec) x9, make 1 in the remaining stitch (9)

31. (dec) x5, make 1 in the remaining stitch (6)

Sew to close.

Arms – In flesh -Make two.

1. 6mr
2. (1, inc) x3 (9)
3-4. Make 1 in each (9)
5. (3, dec) x1, (2, dec) x1 (7)
6-10. Make 1 in each (7)

Finish off flesh colour.

Join White

1. (inc) x7 (14)
2-3. Make 1 in each (14)
4. (dec) x7 (7)

Finish off leaving a length to attach to body later.

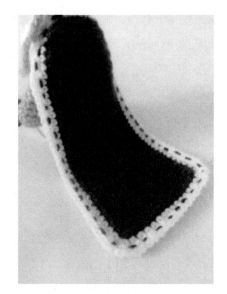

Arm bows – In white – Make two.

1. Chain 13, make 1 in the second chain from the hook and along (12).

Chain 1 and turn your work

2-3. Make 1 in each. Chain 1 turn your work at the end of each row.

Finish off.

Fold in half with the two ends meeting centrally, wrap the wool around the centre a few times to make a bow.

Robe – In purple

1. Chain 16, make 1 in the second from the hook and along. (15). Chain 1 and turn your work

2-28. Make 1 in each, chain 1 and turn your work at the end of each row. (15)

39. (2, dec) x3, make 1 in the remaining 3 stitches (12)

40. Skip the first stitch, (dec, 1) x3, make 1 in the next stitch, leave the remaining stitch of the row unworked.

41. Make 1 stitch around the outside edge of the robe. At each of the four corners make 1 stitch – chain 1 -1 stitch in each.

Finish off purple.

Join white wool.

1-2 Make 1 in each, remember to make a stitch -chain 1 – stitch in each of the four corners.

Finish off white wool.

Using black wool make a running stitch in the white border of the robe in every other stitch.

Crown

In white

1. Chain 49. Make 1 in the second chain from the hook and along (48)

Join with a slip stitch to form a circle, ensure your chain isn't twisted when you slip stitch together.

2-4. Make 1 in each (48)

Finish off white wool

Join gold wool at any point.

1. Make 1 in each (48)

Finish off gold wool.

Join purple wool.

1. Make 1 back post crochet into the gold row above. (48)

2. (3, dec) x10, (dec) x2, make 1 in the remaining stitch (37)

3. Make 1 in each (37)

4. (3, dec) x7, (dec) x1 (29)

5. (2, dec) x7, make 1 in the remaining stitch (22)

6. (2, dec) x5, (dec) x1 (16)

7. (1, dec) x5, make 1 in the remaining stitch (11)

8. (dec) x5, make 1 in the remaining stitch (6)

Finish off, sew shut.

Re-join the gold wool

1. Make 1 in each stitch (48)

2. Chain 21, make 1 in the second chain from the hook and across (20) finish off.

Count 24 stitches around and sew to this point.

Finish off wool.

Count 12 stitches from one of the gold pieces you have just made and chain 21. Make 1 in the second from the hook and across (20). Finish off wool.

Count 24 stitches around and sew in place.

<u>Centre of crown – In gold</u>

1. 6mr

2-3. Make 1 in each (6)

4. (dec) x3

Finish off and sew to the centre of the hat through the gold 'cross' and the purple base.

Using black wool make a running stitch in the white border of the crown in every other stitch.

<u>Hair – In mid brown</u>

1. 6mr

2. (inc) x6 (12)

3. (1, inc) x6 (18)

4. (2, inc) x6 (24)

5. (3, inc) x6 (30)

6. (4, inc) x6 (36)

21

7. (5, inc) x6 (42)

8. (6, inc) x6 (48)

9-14. Make 1 in each (48)

15. Chain 15, slip stitch to the next stitch. Repeat around the edge to form the hair.

Finish off and leave a length of wool to sew to head.

Arm tassels – In gold – Make two

Chain 20, finish off.

Tie two strands to each end of the chain and cut with scissors to make the same length.

Ears – In flesh – Make two

1. 6mr, do not join.

Finish off and leave a length to attach to head.

To Make the staff

I used a slim wooden craft dowel as a base to the staff.

I wrapped in red wool and used a glue gun to secure the ends.

Using gold wool, I rewrapped the dowel leaving the red to show through, again securing with the glue gun.

To make the top of the staff – In gold

1. 6mr

2-3. Make 1 in each (6)

4. (1, dec) x3 (3)

Finish off and glue to the end of the staff.

To make the ball – In red

1. 6mr

2. (inc) x6 (12)

3-4. Make 1 in each (12)

5. (dec) x6 (6)

Finish off, stuff, sew shut.

In yellow.

Chain 13, sew to the ball. Wrap the end around the ball and sew to secure.

Construction.

*Sew the arms to the edge of the body, level with the first row of the dress.

*Sew the robe to the top of the arms.

*Sew the arm bows to the top of the arms.

*Sew the gold tassels in place to the arms. Using end of the gold wool sew a 'V' to the front of the dress.

*Sew the hair to the head. Using the end of the wool, add eyebrows to the face. Sew ears in line with the nose.

*To add the detail to the bottom of the dress, using gold wool, sew in a 'V' around the dress and then alternate the direction of the 'V'

*Sew the crown in place.

* Sew or glue gun the staff and the ball to the hands.

23

HRH The Queen

HRH The Queen

Head – in flesh colour

1. 6mr

2. (inc) x6 (12)

3. (1, inc) x6 (18)

4. (2, inc) x6 (24)

5. (3, inc) x6 (30)

6. (4, inc) x6 (36)

7. (5, inc) x6 (42)

8. (6, inc) x6 (48)

9 – 12. Make 1 stitch in each (48)

13. Make 1 in the next 24 stitches, (P/B) x1, Make 1 in the remaining 23 stitches (48)

14 – 15. Make 1 in each stitch (48)

16. (6, dec) x6 (42)

17. (5, dec) x6 (36)

18. (4, dec) x6 (30)

19. (3, dec) x6 (24)

Finish off flesh colour

Insert eyes at row 11, four spaces apart.

Body - in your chosen colour

1. (4, inc) x5 (30)

2. (5, inc) x5 (35)

3. (6, inc) x5 (40)

4 – 14. Make 1 in each stitch (40)

Stuff the head and body firmly.

15. Turn your work to face away from you and make 1 front post crochet around (40) Chain 1 and turn your work to face the correct way.

16. (6, dec) x5 (35)

17. (3, dec) x7

18. Make 1 s/s in the next four stitches. From this position count 14 stitches around and make 1 s/s

Legs – in flesh colour

1. Join at any point of the leg and 1 make stitch in each around one leg opening (14)

2 -3 Make 1 stitch in each (14)

Finish off wool and repeat for the second leg. Stuff legs lightly.

Shoes – In black

1. 8mr

2. (1, inc) 4 (12)

3 – 4. Make 1 in each stitch (12)

5. Make 1 stitch in the next 8. Chain 1 and turn your work. (8)

6 – 7. Repeat row 5.

Finish off the wool, leaving a long length.

Stuff the shoes and sew to bottom of legs.

to form the legs. Finish off the wool

Coat – in your chosen colour

1. Chain 39.

Make 1 in the second stitch from the hook and across (38)

Chain 1 and turn your work

2 – 14. Make 1 in each, chain 1 turn your work (38)

15. 1 in the first stitch, (4, dec) x6, 1 in the remaining stitch, chain 1 turn your work. (32)

16. (3, dec) x6, make 1 in the remaining stitches, chain 1 and turn your work. (27)

17. Make 1 in each stitch around the outside edge to neaten the edges.

At each corner, make 1 stitch, chain 1, make 1 stitch in each corner.

Finish off the wool and leave a long length to attach to the body.

Add a few stitches to hold in place.

Hat – in your chosen colour

1. 6mr

2. (inc) x6 (12)

3. (1, inc) x6 (18)

4. (2, inc) x6 (24)

5. (3, inc) x6 (30)

6. (4, inc) x6 (36)

7. (5, inc) x6 (42)

8. (6, inc) x6 (48)

9. (7, inc) x6 (54)

10 – 14. Make 1 in each (54)

15. Make 1 FPC in each (54)

16. (2, inc) x18 (72)

17. Make 1 in each (72)

Finish off your work, leaving a long length and attach to head.

Shape the front of the hat.

Gloves/Arms – X2

In white –

1. 8mr

2. (1, inc) x4 (12)

3. Make 1 in each (12)

4. (3, dec) x2, make 1 in the remaining two stitches (10) Finish off.

Join your chosen colour at any point.

1. Make 1FPC around (10)

2 – 8. Make 1 in each (10)

Fold the arms flat and sew across the opening. Se to the side of the coat.

Hair – in light grey

Chain 55.

Make 1 stitch in the 2nd chain from the hook,

* Chain 4, s/s to the base of the chain 4, s/s into the next stitch of the chain*

Repeat from * to * across the length of the chain.

Finish off leaving a long length of wool to attach under the brim of the hat.

Handbag – in black

1. Chain 9, make 1 in the 2nd chain from the hook and along (8) chain 1 and turn your work.

2 -10. Make 1 in each (8) chain 1 and turn your work.

Fold the rectangle you have made in half and make 1 in each around three edges, ensuring the top stays open.

When you have completed three edges and have reached the corner, chain 16, s/s to the opposite corner to form the handle. Finish off the wool.

To make the flower for the hat

In your chosen colours

1. 6mr

Finish off your wool.

Join the second colour at any point and *chain 4, make 1 in the 2nd chain from the hook and the next two stitches. S/s to the base of the chain and s/s to the next stitch. *

Repeat from * to * five more times to make six petals in total.

Construction.

* Add stuffing to the feet and attach to the bottom of the legs.

* Sew the coat to shoulders, sew arms to the side of the body.

* Sew the hat to the head and sew hair around the bottom edge of the hat.

Using the white wool when attaching the hair, make the eyebrows.

*Sew flower to hat.

*Add handbag to the arm, stitch the hands together.

*Add accessories, i.e. flowers, pearl necklace and earrings.

Prince Philip - Retirement

Prince Philip - Retirement

<u>Head – In flesh colour</u>

1. 6mr
2. (INC) x6 (12)
3. (1, inc) x6 (18)
4. (2, inc) x6 (24)
5. (3, inc) x6 (30)
6. (4, inc) x6 (36)
7. (5, inc) x6 (42)
8-14. Make 1 in each (42)
15. 1 in the next 21 stitches, (P/B) x1, 1 in the remaining 20 stitches. (42)
16-17. Make 1 in each. (42)
18. (4, dec) x7, make 1 in remaining stitch (36)
19. Make 1 in each (36)
20. (3, dec) x7 (28)
21. (2, dec) x7 (21)
22. (1, dec) x7 (14)
23-14. Make 1 in each (14)

Finish off flesh colour.

Insert safety eyes at row 12, 3 stitches in-between and stuff the head.

<u>Shirt – in white</u>

Join wool in the previous finish off point.

1. Make 1 in the next 4 stitches, (inc) x1, Make 1 in the next 6 stitches, (inc) x1, Make 1 in the remaining 2 stitches. (16)
2. (2, inc) x5, make 1 in the remaining stitch (21)

3. Make 1 in the next 3 stitches, (inc) x4, Make 1 in the next 9 stitches, (inc) x5 (30)

4-12. Make 1 in each stitch (30)

Finish off white and stuff the body.

Trousers – In black wool

Join wool in the previous finish off point.

1-2. Make 1 in each (30)

3. Make 1 in the next 4 stitches. Count 11 stitches and s/s to form leg one.

4. Make 1 in each (15)

5-16. Make 1 in each (15)

Finish off leg one.

Re-join wool at row 3 to make leg 2, repeat rows 4-16.

Stuff both legs.

Ears – In flesh - Make two

1. 6mr

2. (1, inc) (9)

Finish off, leaving a long tail to attach to head.

Hands – In flesh – Make two

1. 6mr

2. (1, inc) (9)

3-8. Make 1 in each (9)

Finish off flesh colour.

Arms – In chosen colour

Repeat for both arms.

Join at previous finish off point of flesh colour for hands.

1. Make 1 in each (9)

2. (1, inc) x4, 1 (13)

3. Make 1 in the next 12 stitches, (inc) x1 in the last stitch. (15)

4-7. Make 1 in each (15)

Finish off sleeve colour, leaving a tail to attach to body later.

Coat - In chosen colour.

1. Chain 29, Make 1 in the second chain from the hook and along (28)

2-17. Make 1 in each (28)

18. Make 1 in the next 5 stitches, (dec) x3, make 1 in the next five stitches, (dec) x3, make 1 in the remaining five stitches (21)

19. Make 1 in the next 4 stitches, (dec) x2, make 1 in the next 6 stitches, (dec) x 2, make 1 in the remaining 4 stitches. (18)

20. In the first stitch of the row make 5 stitches, make 1 in the next 16 stitches, make 5 in the last stitch of the round. (26- including the two groups of five stitches)

21.Make 1 stitch around the edge of the coat (At each corner make 1 stitch a chain 1 and a stitch in the same corner stitch.)

Collar – In white

1. Chain 17, make 1 in the second chain from the hook and along (16)

2. In the first stitch make 3 stitches, make 1 in the rest of the row, in the last stitch make 3 stitches.

Finish off, leave a length of wool to attach to neck later.

Tie – In black

1. 8mr

2. Chain 8. Skip the first stitch and make 1 in the remaining stitches to form the tie.

Finish off, leaving a length of wool to attach to the neck later.

Shoes – In black – Make two

1. 8mr

2. (1, inc) x4 (12)

3-4. Make 1 in each (12)

5. Make 1 in the next 8 stitches, chain 1 turn your work. (8)

6-8. Repeat row 5.

Finish off, leave a length of wool.

Sew the heel together using s/s on each shoe.

Bowler hat – In black

1. 6mr

2. (inc) x6 (12)

3. (1, inc) x6 (18)

4. (2, inc) x6 (24)

5. (3, inc) x6 (30)

6. (4, inc) x6 (36)

7. (5, inc) x6 (42)

8. (6, inc) x6 (48)

9-11. Make 1 in each (48)

12. Make 1 in the next 20 stitches, (dec, 1) x2, (2, dec) x1 (46)

13. Make 1 in each (46)

14. Make 1 front post crochet around in each (46)

15. Make 1 in each. (46)

Finish off black wool, leaving a length of wool to attach to head.

Construction.

*Lightly add stuffing to the feet and sew to the bottom of the legs.

*Sew the tie to the front centre of the neck.

*Sew the collar to the neck.

*To attach the coat, place onto the shoulders of your Prince Philip and sew the collars down in place. Add a few stitches around the neck to hold in place.

*Add the arms to the sides of the body. I prefer to sew my arms to three rows from the top of the coat, but of course you can place them in your preferred position.

*Sew the ears to the head at rows 13-15, in line with the nose.

*Sew the hat in place to secure.

*Using a little white wool add eyebrows and sideburns to finish off your Prince Philip in his retirement outfit.

Prince Philip
Military outfit

Prince Philip Military outfit

Head – In flesh colour

1. 6mr
2. (INC) x6 (12)
3. (1, inc) x6 (18)
4. (2, inc) x6 (24)
5. (3, inc) x6 (30)
6. (4, inc) x6 (36)
7. (5, inc) x6 (42)
8-14. Make 1 in each (42)
15. 1 in the next 21 stitches, (P/B) x1, 1 in the remaining 20 stitches. (42)
16-17. Make 1 in each. (42)
18. (4, dec) x7, make 1 in the remaining stitch (36)
19. Make 1 in each (36)
20. (3, dec) x7 (28)
21. (2, dec) x7 (21)
22. (1, dec) x7 (14)
23-14. Make 1 in each (14)

Finish off flesh colour.

Insert safety eyes at row 12, 3 stitches in-between and stuff the head.

Shirt – in white

Join wool in the previous finish off point.

1. Make 1 in the next 4 stitches, (inc) x1, Make 1 in the next 6 stitches,

(inc) x1, Make 1 in the remaining 2 stitches. (16)

2. (2, inc) x5, make 1 in the remaining stitch (21)

3. Make 1 in the next 3 stitches, (inc) x4, Make 1 in the next 9 stitches, (inc) x5 (30)

4-12. Make 1 in each stitch (30)

Finish off white and stuff the body.

Trousers – In black wool

Join wool in the previous finish off point.

1-2. Make 1 in each (30)

3. Make 1 in the next 4 stitches. Count 11 stitches and s/s to form leg one.

4. Make 1 in each (15)

5-16. Make 1 in each (15)

Finish off leg one.

Re-join wool at row 3 to make leg 2, repeat rows 4-16.

Stuff both legs.

Ears – In flesh - Make two

1. 6mr

2. (1, inc) (9)

Finish off, leaving a long tail to attach to head.

Hands – In flesh – Make two

1. 6mr

2. (1, inc) (9)

3-8. Make 1 in each (9)

Finish off flesh colour.

Arms – In red

Repeat for both arms.

Join at previous finish off point of flesh colour for hands.

1. Make 1 in each (9)

2. (1, inc) x4, 1 (13)

3. Make 1 in the next 12 stitches, (inc) x1 in the last stitch. (15)

4-12. Make 1 in each (15)

13. (dec) x7, make 1 in the remaining stitch.

Finish off, leaving a length of wool to attach to body later.

Shoes – In black – Make two

1. 8mr

2. (1, inc) x4 (12)

3-4. Make 1 in each (12)

5. Make 1 in the next 8 stitches, chain 1 turn your work. (8)

6-8. Repeat row 5.

Finish off, leave a length of wool.

Jacket – In red

1. Chain 40, make 1 in the second chain form the hook and along (39) Chain 1 and turn your work.

2-12. Make 1 in each, (39), chain 1 and turn your work at the end of each row.

13. Make 1 in the next 7 stitches, (dec) x3, make 1 in the next 12 stitches, (dec) x3, make 1 in the remaining 7 stitches. (32)

14. Make 1 in the next 6 stitches, (dec) x2, make 1 in the next 12 stitches, (dec) x2, make 1 in the remaining 6 stitches (28)

15. Make 1 in each around the edge of the jacket, at each of the four corners make '1 stitch – chain 1- 1 stitch' in each.

Finish off red.

Join yellow.

1-3. Make 1 in each. (28)

Finish off yellow.

Join white wool.

Make 1 in each around three edges of the jacket, *do not crochet along the bottom of the jacket*.

In each of the corners make

'1 stitch – chain 1 – 1 stitch' in each.

Finish off white wool.

Shoulder patches – in yellow- Make two.

1. Chain 3, make 1 in the second chain from the hook and the next, chain one and turn your work. (2)

2—6. Make 1 in each (2)

7. Make 1 in each around the edge of the shoulder patch, in each corner make '1 stitch – chain 1 -1 stitch'

Finish off and leave a length of wool to attach to shoulders later.

Sash – in blue

1. Chain 4, make 1 in the second chain from the hook and across (3) Chain one and turn your work.

2-27. Make 1 in each (3)

28. Make 1 in each around the edge of the sash, in each corner make '1 stitch – chain 1 – 1 stitch'

Finish off, leaving a length to attach to the body later.

To make the medals.

Using red, yellow and blue felt, cut and glue gun small pieces together.

See photo below

To make chain.

Using yellow wool, chain 20. Finish off and leave a length of wool to attach to body later.

Hair – In white.

1. Chain 16, make 1 in the second chain from the hook and each across, (15), chain 1 and turn your work

2. (inc) x1, make 1 in the next 13 stitches, (inc) x1 (17)

3. (inc) x1, make 1 in the next 15 stitches, (inc) x1 (19)

4. (inc) x1, make 1 in the next 17 stitches, (inc) x1 (21)

5-9. Make 1 in each (21)

10. (2, dec) x5 (15)

11. (2, dec) x3, make 1 in the remaining 3 stitches. (12)

12. (2, dec) x2, make 1 in the remaining 3 stitches (9)

13. (1, dec) x3 (6)

14-15. Make 1 stitch in each around the edge of the hair.

Finish off leaving a length of wool to attach to head.

Construction.

*Lightly add stuffing to the feet and sew to the bottom of the legs.

*To attach the coat, place onto the shoulders of your Prince Philip and sew the collars down in place. Add a few stitches around the neck to hold in place.

*Add the arms to the sides of the body. I joined the hands behind his back as Prince Philip often stood this way.

*Sew the hair to the back of the head, using a little white wool add eyebrows and sideburns to finish off your Prince Philip in his military outfit.

*Sew or glue gun the medals in position on the chest.

Prince Charles

Prince Charles

Head – in flesh colour

1. 6mr
2. (INC) x6 (12)
3. (1, inc) x6 (18)
4. (2, inc) x6 (24)
5. (3, inc) x6 (30)
6. (4, inc) x6 (36)
7. (5, inc) x6 (42)
8-14. Make 1 in each (42)
15. 1 in the next 21 stitches, (P/B) x1, 1 in the remaining 20 stitches. (42)
16-17. Make 1 in each. (42)
18. (4, dec) x7, make 1 in remaining stitch (36)
19. Make 1 in each (36)
20. (3, dec) x7 (28)
21. (2, dec) x7 (21)
22. (1, dec) x7 (14)
23-14. Make 1 in each (14)

Finish off flesh colour.

Insert safety eyes at row 12, 3 stitches in-between and stuff the head.

Body – In black

1. Make 1 in the next 5, (inc) x1, make 1 in the next 7, (inc) x1 (16)
2. (2, inc) x5, make 1 in the remaining stitch (21)
3. Make 1 in the next 8, (inc) x3, make 1 in the next 7, (inc) x3 (27)
4. (10, inc) x1, (14, inc) x1, make 1 in the remaining stitch (29)
5-14. Make 1 in each (29)
15. (5, dec) x1, count 14 stitches around and slip stitch into this stitch, make 1 in the remaining 8 and slip stitch to the first stitch of the round.

To form legs

16-29. Make 1 in each (14)

Finish off wool and re-join to form leg two, repeat rows 16-29.

Hair – In grey

1. Chain 16, make 1 in the second chain from the hook and each across, (15), chain 1 and turn your work

2. (inc) x1, make 1 in the next 13 stitches, (inc) x1 (17)

3. (inc) x1, make 1 in the next 15 stitches, (inc) x1 (19)

4. (inc) x1, make 1 in the next 17 stitches, (inc) x1 (21)

5-9. Make 1 in each (21)

10. (2, dec) x5 (15)

11. (2, dec) x3, make 1 in the remaining 3 stitches. (12)

12. (2, dec) x2, make 1 in the remaining 3 stitches (9)

13. (1, dec) x3 (6)

14-15. Make 1 stitch in each around the edge of the hair.

Finish off leaving a length of wool to attach to head.

Jacket – In black

1. Chain 35, make 1 in the second chain from the hook and along, (34), chain 1 and turn your work.

2-10. Make 1 in each (34)

11. Make 1 in the next 10, (dec) x2, make 1 in the next 2 stitches, (dec) x1, make 1 in the next 5 stitches, (dec) x2, make 1 in the remaining 10 (29)

12-16. Make 1 in each (29)

17. Make 1 in the next 6, (dec) x3, make 1 in the next 5, (dec) x3, make 1 in the remaining 6 (23)

18. Make 1 in the next 5, (dec) x2, make 1 in the next 5, (dec) x2, make 1 in the remaining 5 (19)

19-22. Make 1 in each (19)

23. Make 1 in each around the edge of the jacket. At each corner make '1 stitch – chain 1 – 1 stitch'

24. Repeat row 23.

Finish off wool leaving a tail to attach the jacket later to body.

Trouser stripe – In red – Make two.

Chain 17, make 1 in the second chain from the hook and along (16)

Finish off leaving a length of wool to attach to the legs.

Sash – In blue

1. Chain 4, make 1 in the second from the hook and the next 2. (3)

Chain 1 and turn your work.

2-27. Make 1 in each (3)

28. Make 1 in each around the edge of the sash, at each corner make '1 stitch – chain 1 – 1 stitch'

Finish off wool leaving a length of wool to attach to shoulder later.

Shoulder plates – In yellow – Make two.

1. Chain 3, make 1 in the second from the hook and the next (2)

Chain 1 and turn your work.

2-6. Make 1 in each (3)

7. Make 1 in each around the edge of the shoulder plate, in each corner make '1 stitch – chain 1 -1 stitch'

Finish off wool, leaving a length of wool to attach to shoulders later.

Breast chain – In yellow

Chain 28. Finish off leaving a length of wool to attach.

Belt

In yellow –

1. Chain 35, make 1 in the second from the hook and along (34)

Finish off yellow wool.

In red –

2. Make 1 in each (34)

Finish off red wool

In yellow –

3. Make 1 in each (34)

Finish off leaving a length to attach to waist later.

Hands – In flesh – Make two.

1. 6mr
2. (1, inc) x3 (9)
3-8. Make 1 in each (9)

Finish off wool.

Arms – In black.

1. Join black wool to row 7 of the hands and make 1 front post crochet around in each (9)
2-4. Make 1 in each (9)
5. (2, inc) x3 (12)
6-7. Make 1 in each (12)
8. Make 1 in the next 10, (inc) x2 (14)
9-11. Make 1 in each (14)

Finish off the black wool, leave a length of wool to attach to the body later.

At the bottom of the sleeves, using yellow wool, make three bands.

Hat

In black –

1. Chain 45, make 1 in the second chain from the hook and along. (44)

Join with a slip stitch to form a circle, ensure your work is not twisted before you join.

Finish off black wool.

In red-

2-4. Make 1 in each (44)

Finish off red wool.

In black –

5. Make 1 in each (44)

6. Make 1 in the next 26, chain 1 and turn your work. (26)

7. Skip the first stitch, make 1 in the next 6, slip stitch into the remaining stitch. (7)

Chain 1 turn your work.

8. Make 1 in the next 7, make 2 slip stitches back down the edge to row 6 and make 1 in the next 18 stitches.

9. Continue to complete a full round of the hat, making 1 stitch in each (44)

10. Make 1 front post crochet in each (44)

11. (1, inc) x9, make 1 in the next 8, (inc, 1) x9, make 1 in the remaining stitch (63)

12. (2, inc) x9, make 1 in the next 8, (inc, 2) x9, make 1 in the remaining stitch (81)

13. Make 1 in each (81)

14. (8, dec) x8 (72)

15. (7, dec) x8 (64)

16. (2, dec) x16 (48)

17. (2, dec) x12 (36)

18. (2, dec) x9 (27)

19. (1, dec) x9, make 1 in the remaining stitch (19)

20. (1, dec) x6, make 1 in the remaining stitch (13)

21. (dec) x6, make 1 in the remaining stitch (7)

Finish off and sew shut

Hat peak – In black.

1. Chain 13, make 1 in the second from the hook and along (12), chain 1 and turn your work

2. Make 1 in each (12) chain 1 and turn your work

3. Skip the first stitch, make 1 in the next 10, leave the last stitch of the row unworked (10), chain 1 and turn your work

4. Skip the first stitch, make 1 in the next 8 stitches, leave the last stitch unworked (8)

5. Make 1 in each around the edge of the peak. Finish off and sew to the front of the hat.

Hat detail – In yellow – Make two.

Chain 12. Finish off and sew to the hat peak.

Ears – In flesh - Make two

1. 6mr

2. (1, inc) (9)

Finish off, leaving a long tail to attach to head.

Shoes – In black – Make two.

1. 8mr

2. (1, inc) x4 (12)

3-5. Make 1 in each (12)

5. Make 1 in the next 8 stitches, chain 1 turn your work. (8)

6-8. Repeat row 5.

Finish off, leave a length of wool.

To make the medals.

Using red, yellow and blue felt, cut and glue gun small pieces together.

Construction.

*Lightly add stuffing to the feet and sew to the bottom of the legs.

*To attach the coat, place onto the shoulders of your Prince Charles and sew the collar in place. Add a few stitches around the neck to hold in place.

*Add the arms to the sides of the body. I prefer to sew my arms to three rows from the top of the coat, but of course you can place them in your preferred position.

*Sew the ears to the head at rows 13-15, in line with the nose.

*Sew hair to head in the position you prefer.

Using a little grey wool add eyebrows and sideburns.

*Sew the sash to the right shoulder.

* Sew the shoulder plates to each arm, on the right-hand side, use the shoulder pad to cover the sash.

*Sew the chest chain in place

* Sew the belt around the waist, ensure the blue sash is under the belt.

* Sew the red trouser stripes to the outside edge of the legs.

*Glue gun or sew your medals to Princes Charles' chest.

Camilla

Camilla

<u>Head – In flesh colour</u>

1. 6mr

2. (inc) x6 (12)

3. (1, inc) x6 (18)

4. (2, inc) x6 (24)

5. (3, inc) x6 (30)

6. (4, inc) x6 (36)

7. (5, inc) x6 (42)

8. (6, inc) x6 (48)

9 – 12. Make 1 stitch in each (48)

13. Make 1 in the next 24 stitches, (P/B) x1, Make 1 in the remaining 23 stitches (48)

14 – 15. Make 1 in each stitch (48)

16. (6, dec) x6 (42)

17. (5, dec) x6 (36)

18. (4, dec) x6 (30)

19. (3, dec) x6 (24)

20. (2, dec) x6 (18)

21. (1, dec) x6 (12)

Insert eyes at row 11 with five stitches in-between and stuff the head.

22-23. Make 1 in each (12)

24.(1, inc) x1, make 1 in the next 3, (inc) x1, make 1 in the remaining 6 stitches (14)

25. Make 1 in the next 3 stitches, (inc) x2, Make 1 in the next 7 stitches, (inc) x2 (18)

26. Make 1 in each stitch (18).

Finish off flesh colour.

Top - In white

1. (8, inc) x1, (inc, 2), (inc) x2, make 1 in the remaining stitches (20)

2. Make 1 in the next 10 stitches, (inc,2) x2, (inc) x2, make 1 in the next 2 stitches, (inc) x2, make 1 each in the remaining stitches (26)

3-4. Make 1 in each (26)

5. Make 1 in the next 11, (dec) x6, make 1 in the remaining 3 stitches (20)

6-7. Make 1 in each (20)

Finish off white wool.

Join pale pink, in the previous finish off point.

8. (inc) x2, make 1 in the next 6 stitches, (inc) x2, make 1 in the remaining 10 stitches (24)

9. (inc) x2, make 1 in the next 8 stitches, (inc) x2, make 1 in the remaining 11 stitches (27)

10-11. Make 1 in each (27)

12. Make 1 in the next 26, in the last stitch make (inc) x1 (28)

13. Make 1 in each (28)

14. Turn your work to face away from you and make 1 front post crochet around. (28)

15. Turn your work the correct way of working.

Make 1 in the next 7 stitches, count 14 stitches around and make a slip stitch to form the leg holes. Continue making another 1 in each for the next 7 and join to the first slip stitch.

Continue making 1 stitch in the next 7 to finish the round.

Finish off pale pink wool, stuff body.

Legs – In flesh colour

Repeat for each leg

1. Join at any point of row 15 and make 1 in each (14)

2-4. Make 1in each (14)

Finish off and stuff the legs.

Skirt edging – In pale pink.

Re-join the wool on row 13 and make 1 in each around for two rows. (28)

Finish off wool.

Shoes – In pale pink - Make two.

1. 8mr

2. (1, inc) x4 (12)

3-5. Make 1 in each (12)

6. Make 1 in the next 8 stitches, chain 1 and turn your work (8)

7-8. Make 1 in each (8)

Finish off wool and slip stitch the heel together to form the shoes. Leave a length of wool to attach to the legs.

Coat – In pale pink

1. Chain 25, make 1 in the second chain from the hook and along (24).

Chain 1 and turn your work.

2-8. Make 1 in each (24)

9. (4, dec) x4 (20)

10-17. Make 1 in each (20)

18. Make 1 in the next 4 stitches, (dec) x2, make 1 in the next 4, (dec) x2, make 1 in the remaining four stitches (16)

19. Make 1 in each (16)

20. Make 1 in each around the outside of the coat, at each corner make '1 stitch – chain 1 – 1 stitch'

Chain 1 and turn your work

21. Repeat row 20

22. Make 5 stitches in to the first stitch, make 1 in each for 16 stitches, make 5 stitches into the next stitch.

Continue around the rest of the jacket, making 1 in each.

Finish off wool, leaving a length to attach jacket to body.

Hands – In flesh – Make two.
1. 6mr
2. (1, inc) x3 (9)
3-8. Make 1 in each (9)
Finish off wool.

Arms – In Pale pink.
1. Join wool to row 7 of the hands and make 1 front post crochet around in each (9)
2-4. Make 1 in each (9)
5. (2, inc) x3 (12)
6-7. Make 1 in each (12)
8. Make 1 in the next 10 (inc) x2 (14)
9. Make 1 in each (14)
Finish off the wool, leave a length of wool to attach to the body later.

Hair – In white.
1. 6mr
2. (inc) x6 (12)
3. (1, inc) x6 (18)
4. (2, inc) x6 (24)
5. (3, inc) x6 (30)
6. (4, inc) x6 (36)
7. (5, inc) x6 (42)
8. (6, inc) x6 (48)
9-14. Make 1 in each (48)

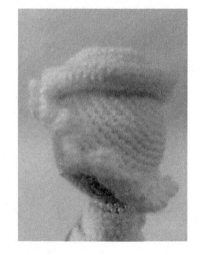

15. Chain 12, slip stitch to the next stitch. Repeat around the edge to form the hair.
Finish off and leave a length of wool to sew to head.

Ears – In flesh – Make two

1. 6mr, do not join.

Finish off and leave a length to attach to head.

Hat – In pale pink.

1. 6mr

2. (inc) x6 (12)

3. (1, inc) x6 (24)

4. (2, inc) x6 (30)

5. (3, inc) x6 (36)

6. (4, inc) x6 (36)

7. (5, inc) x6 (42)

8. Make 1 back loop stitch in each (42)

9-13. Make 1 in each stitch (42)

14. Make 1 front post stitch in each (42)

15. (6, inc) x6 (48)

16. (7, inc) x 6 (54)

17. (8, inc) x6 (60)

18. (9, inc) x6 (66)

19. (10, inc) x2, make 1 in the next 22 stitches, (10, inc) x2 (70)

20. (10, dec) x5, make 1 in the remaining 10 stitches. (66)

Finish off your work, leave a length of wool to sew to head.

Hat flower

In dusky pink

1. 6mr

2. (inc) x6 (12)

3. (dec) x6 (6)

Finish off.

Join pale pink

Chain 6, make a slip stitch into the next stitch.

Repeat a total of six times.

Finish off.

Join dusky pink.

Chain 6, make a slip stitch into the next stitch.

Repeat a total of six times.

Finish off leaving a length of wool to attach to hat.

Construction,

*Lightly stuff the feet and sew to legs.

*Sew hair to head, using the white wool, add eyebrows to face.

*Sew the ears to the head, under the hair and in line with the ears.

*Sew hat to head, Add the flower.

*Lightly stuff the feet ad sew to the bottom of legs.

* Sew coat to shoulders, bend collar and secure in place with a few stitches.

* Sew arms to the side of the body.

* Add accessories, i.e. earrings and necklace.

Prince William

Prince William

<u>Head – in flesh colour</u>

1. 6mr
2. (INC) x6 (12)
3. (1, inc) x6 (18)
4. (2, inc) x6 (24)
5. (3, inc) x6 (30)
6. (4, inc) x6 (36)
7. (5, inc) x6 (42)
8-14. Make 1 in each (42)
15. 1 in the next 21 stitches, (P/B) x1, 1 in the remaining 20 stitches. (42)
16-17. Make 1 in each. (42)
18. (4, dec) x7, make 1 in the remining stitch (36)
19. Make 1 in each (36)
20. (3, dec) x7 (28)
21. (2, dec) x7 (21)
22. (1, dec) x7 (14)
23-14. Make 1 in each for the next 12, (inc) x2 (16)

Finish off flesh colour.

Insert safety eyes at row 12, 3 stitches in-between and stuff the head.

<u>Body – In white.</u>

1. Make 1 in the next 5, (inc) x1, make 1 in the next 9, (inc) x1 (18)
2. (2, inc) x6 (24)
3. Make 1 in the next 10, (inc) x2, make 1 in the next 10, (inc) x2 (28)
4. (11, inc) x1, (15, inc) x1 (30)
5-14. Make 1 in each (30)

Finish off white.

Join grey/blue wool.

15-16. Make 1 in each stitch (30)

Stuff the body.

To form legs.

17. Make 1 in the next 8 stitches, count 15 stitches and make a slip stitch into the stitch.

Make 1 stitch around to form the first leg, slip stitch into previous slip stitch.

Finish the first leg by making 1 stitch into the next 7 stitches. (15)

18-30. Make 1 in each (14)

Finish off wool and re-join to form leg two, repeat rows 18-30.

Stuff both legs.

Jacket – In grey/blue

1. Chain 35, make 1 in the second chain from the hook and along, (34), chain 1 and turn your work.

2-10. Make 1 in each (34)

11. Make 1 in the next 10, (dec) x2, make 1 in the next 5 stitches, (dec) x2, make 1 in the remaining 10 (29)

12-16. Make 1 in each (29)

17. Make 1 in the next 6, (dec) x3, make 1 in the next 5, (dec) x3, make 1 in the remaining 6 (23)

18. Make 1 in the next 5, (dec) x2, make 1 in the next 5, (dec) x2, make 1 in the remaining 5 (19)

19-21. Make 1 in each (19)

22. Make 1 in each around the edge of the jacket. At each corner make '1 stitch – chain 1 – 1 stitch'

24. Make 5 in the first stitch, slip stitch x1, make 1 in the next 16, slip stitch x1, make 5 stitches in the next. Continue making 1 stitch in each to complete round 24.

Finish off wool leaving a tail to attach the jacket later to body.

Hands – In flesh – Make two

1. 6mr
2. (1, inc) (9)
3-8. Make 1 in each (9)

Finish off flesh colour.

Arms – In grey/blue – Make two

1. Join black wool to row 7 of the hands and make 1 front post crochet around in each (9)
2-4. Make 1 in each (9)
5. (2, inc) x3 (12)
6-7. Make 1 in each (12)
8. Make 1 in the next 10, (inc) x2 (14)
9-11. Make 1 in each (14)

Finish off the black wool, leave a length of wool to attach to the body later.

At the bottom of the sleeves, using yellow wool, make three bands.

Shoes – In black – Make two

1. 8mr
2. (1, inc) x4 (12)
3-4. Make 1 in each (12)
5. Make 1 in the next 8 stitches, chain 1 turn your work. (8)
6-8. Repeat row 5.

Finish off, leave a length of wool.

Sew the heel together using s/s on each shoe.

Collar – In white

1. Chain 21, make 1 in the second chain from the hook and along (20)

2. In the first stitch make 3 stitches, make 1 in the rest of the row, in the last stitch make 3 stitches.

Finish off, leave a length of wool to attach to neck later.

Tie – In black.

1. 8mr

2. Chain 8. Skip the first stitch and make 1 in the remaining stitches to form the tie.

Finish off, leaving a length of wool to attach to the neck later.

Sash – In pale blue

1. Chain 4, make 1 in the second from the hook and the next 2. (3)

Chain 1 and turn your work.

2-27. Make 1 in each (3)

28. Make 1 in each around the edge of the sash, at each corner make '1 stitch – chain 1 – 1 stitch'

Finish off wool leaving a length of wool to attach to shoulder later.

Shoulder plates – In blue – Make two.

1. Chain 3, make 1 in the second from the hook and the next (2)

Chain 1 and turn your work.

2-6. Make 1 in each (3)

7. Make 1 in each around the edge of the shoulder plate, in each corner make '1 stitch – chain 1 -1 stitch'

Finish off wool, leaving a length of wool to attach to shoulders later.

Breast chain – In yellow

Chain 28. Finish off leaving a length of wool to attach.

Belt

In yellow –

1. Chain 35, make 1 in the second from the hook and along (34)

Finish off yellow wool.

In blue –

2. Make 1 in each (34)

Finish off red wool

In yellow –

3. Make 1 in each (34)

Finish off leaving a length to attach to waist later.

Ears – In flesh - Make two

1. 6mr

2. (1, inc) (9)

Finish off, leaving a long tail to attach to head.

Hair – In light brown

1. Chain 16, make 1 in the second chain from the hook and each across, (15), chain 1 and turn your work

2. (inc) x1, make 1 in the next 13 stitches, (inc) x1 (17)

3. (inc) x1, make 1 in the next 15 stitches, (inc) x1 (19)

4. (inc) x1, make 1 in the next 17 stitches, (inc) x1 (21)

5-9. Make 1 in each (21)

10. (2, dec) x5 (15)

11. (2, dec) x3, make 1 in the remaining 3 stitches. (12)

12. (2, dec) x2, make 1 in the remaining 3 stitches (9)

13. (1, dec) x3 (6)

14-15. Make 1 stitch in each around the edge of the hair.

Finish off leaving a length of wool to attach to head.

To make the medals.

Using red, yellow and blue felt, cut and glue gun small pieces together.

Construction.

*Lightly stuff the feet and sew to the legs.

*Sew tie to neck and add collar.

*Sew jacket to the shoulders, add the arms to the side of the body.

*Sew the sash to the right shoulder and the chain to the left. Sew the shoulder panels to the arms to cover the sash and chain ends.

*Sew belt to the waist, ensure the sash is under the belt before fixing.

*Sew hair to the head, using the brown wool, add eyebrows and sideburns.

*Add ears to the head, below hairline, in line with the nose.

*Sew or glue medals to chest on the sash.

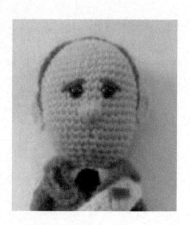

Katherine

Katherine

Head - In flesh colour

1. 6mr
2. (inc) x6 (12)
3. (1, inc) x6 (18)
4. (2, inc) x6 (24)
5. (3, inc) x6 (30)
6. (4, inc) x6 (36)
7. (5, inc) x6 (42)
8. (6, inc) x6 (48)
9 – 12. Make 1 stitch in each (48)
13. Make 1 in the next 24 stitches, (P/B) x1, Make 1 in the remaining 23 stitches (48)
14 – 15. Make 1 in each stitch (48)
16. (6, dec) x6 (42)
17. (5, dec) x6 (36)
18. (4, dec) x6 (30)
19. (3, dec) x6 (24)
20. (2, dec) x6 (18)
21. (1, dec) x6 (12)

Insert eyes at row 11 with five stitches in-between and stuff the head.

22-23. Make 1 in each (12)
24.(inc, 1) x1, make 1 in the next 3, (inc) x1, make 1 in the remaining 6 stitches (14)
25. Make 1 in the next 4 stitches, (inc) x2, Make 1 in the next 6 stitches, (inc) x2 (18)
26. Make 1 in each stitch (18).
Finish off flesh colour.

Dress - In pale blue

Joint blue in the previous finish off point.

1. (6, inc) x1, make 1 in the next 2 stitches, (inc) x4, make 1 in the remaining 5 stitches (23)

2. Make 1 in the next 10 stitches, (inc,3, inc) x1, make 1 in the next 3 stitches, (3, inc, 2) (26)

3-4. Make 1 in each (26)

5. Make 1 in the next 11, (dec) x6, make 1 in the remaining 3 stitches (20)

6-7. Make 1 in each (20)

8. Make 1 in the next 7 stitches, (inc) x3, make 1 in the next 7 stitches, (inc) x3 (26)

9. (10, inc) x1, (11, inc) x1, make 1 in the remaining 3 stitches (28)

10-14. Make 1 in each (28)

15. Turn your work to face away from you and make 1 front post crochet around. (28)

16. Turn your work the correct way of working.

Make 1 in the next 5 stitches, count 14 stitches around and make a slip stitch to form the leg holes. Continue making another 1 in each for the next 14 and join to the first slip stitch, continue making 1 stitch in the next 7 to finish the round. (28)

Finish off wool and stuff the body.

Legs – In flesh colour

Repeat for each leg

1. Join at any point of row 14 and make 1 in each (14)

2. (4, dec) x2, make 1 in the last 2 remaining stitches (12)

3-5. Make 1in each (12)

67

Finish off and stuff the legs.

Skirt edging – In blue.
Re-join the wool on row 13 and make 1 in each around for two rows. (28)
Finish off wool.

Shoes – In blue - Make two.
1. 8mr
2. (1, inc) x4 (12)
3-5. Make 1 in each (12)
6. Make 1 in the next 8 stitches, chain 1 and turn your work (8)
7-8. Make 1 in each (8)
Finish off wool and slip stitch the heel together to form the shoes. Leave a length of wool to attach to the legs.

Hands – In flesh – Make two.
1. 6mr
2. (1, inc) x3 (9)
3-8. Make 1 in each (9)
Finish off wool.

Arms – In blue.
1. Join wool to row 7 of the hands and make 1 front post crochet around in each (9)
2-5 Make 1 in each (9)
Finish off the wool, leave a length of wool to attach to the body later.

Collar – In blue.
1. Chain 22, make 1 in the second chain from the hook and along (21)

2. (inc) x1, make 1 in each for 19, (inc) x1 (23)

3. (inc) x1, make 1 in each for 21 stitches, (inc) x1 (25)

Finish off, leave a length of wool to sew to neckline.

Hair – In dark brown.

1. 6mr

2. (inc) x6 (12)

3. (1, inc) x6 (18)

4. (2, inc) x6 (24)

5. (3, inc) x6 (30)

6. (4, inc) x6 (36)

7. (5, inc) x6 (42)

8. (6, inc) x6 (48)

9-14. Make 1 in each (48)

Finish off and leave a length of wool to sew to head.

For hair bun – In dark brown.

1. 6mr

2. (inc) x6 (12)

3. (1, inc) x6 (18)

4. (2, inc) x6 (24)

5. (3, inc) x6 (30)

6. Make 1 in each (30)

7. (3, dec) x6 (24)

8. (2, dec) x6 (18)

Finish off and leave a length of wool to sew to the back of the head.

Hair edge – In dark brown

1. Chain 49, make 1 in the second chain from the hook and along (48)

2. Make 1 in the next 23, slip stitch into the next 2 stitches, make 1 each in the remaining 23 (48)

Finish off and leave a length of wool to sew the head, overlapping the hairline around the head.

Ears – In flesh – Make two

1. 6mr, do not join.

Finish off and leave a length to attach to head.

 Hat – In blue

1. 6mr

2. (inc) x6 (12)

3. (1, inc) x6 (18)

4. (2, inc) x6 (24)

5-6 Make 1 in each (24)

7. (3, inc) x6 (30)

8. (2, dec) x7, make 1 each in the remaining stitches (23)

9. (1, dec) x7, (dec) x1 (15)

Finish off and leave a length of wool to sew to head.

Flower for hat – In white

1. 8mr

2. *Make 1 puffball stitch in the first stitch, slip stitch to the next stitch*

Repeat * to * to make a total of four petals. Finish off white wool.

Hat chain – In blue.

Chain 30 and finish off.

Fold in half and sew to the hat at the back of the flower.

Construction.

*Sew hair to the head, bun to the bottom of the hair. Sew the hair edge around the hairline. Using the brown wool add eyebrows.

* Sew the arms to the body and the collar around the neckline.

* Lightly stuff the feet and sew to the legs.

*Sew hat to the head, add flower and the hat chain.

* Add accessories, i.e. earrings and brooch.

Prince Harry

Prince Harry

Head – in flesh colour

1. 6mr
2. (inc) x6 (12)
3. (1, inc) x6 (18)
4. (2, inc) x6 (24)
5. (3, inc) x6 (30)
6. (4, inc) x6 (36)
7. (5, inc) x6 (42)
8-14. Make 1 in each (42)
15. 1 in the next 21 stitches, (P/B) x1, 1 in the remaining 20 stitches. (42)
16-17. Make 1 in each. (42)
18. (4, dec) x7, make 1 in the remaining stitch (36)
19. Make 1 in each (36)
20. (3, dec) x7 (28)
21. (2, dec) x7 (21)
22. (1, dec) x7 (14)
23-14. Make 1 in each for the next 12, (inc) x2 (16)

Finish off flesh colour.

Insert safety eyes at row 12, 3 stitches in-between and stuff the head.

Body – In white.

1. Make 1 in the next 5, (inc) x1, make 1 in the next 9, (inc) x1 (18)
2. (2, inc) x6 (24)
3. Make 1 in the next 10, (inc) x2, make 1 in the next 10, (inc) x2 (28)
4. (11, inc) x1, (15, inc) x1 (30)
5-14. Make 1 in each (30)

Finish off white.

Join blue wool.

15-16. Make 1 in each stitch (30)

Stuff the body.

To form legs.

17. Make 1 in the next 8 stitches, count 15 stitches and make a slip stitch into the stitch.

Make 1 stitch around to form the first leg, slip stitch into previous slip stitch.

Finish the first leg by making 1 stitch into the next 7 stitches. (15)

18-30. Make 1 in each (14)

Finish off wool and re-join to form leg two, repeat rows 18-30.

Stuff both legs.

Jacket – In blue

1. Chain 35, make 1 in the second chain from the hook and along, (34), chain 1 and turn your work.

2-12. Make 1 in each (34)

13. Make 1 in the next 10, (dec) x2, make 1 in the next 2 stitches, (dec) x1, make 1 in the next 6 stitches, (dec) x2, make 1 in the remaining 10 (30)

14. Make 1 in the next 6, (dec) x3, make 1 in the next 7, (dec) x3, make 1 in the remaining 6 (26)

15. Make 1 in the next 5, (dec) x2, make 1 in the next 6, (dec) x2, make 1 in the remaining 5 (19)

16. Make 1 in each around the edge of the jacket. At each corner make '1 stitch – chain 1 – 1 stitch'

Chain 1 and turn your work.

24. Make 5 stitches in the first stitch, make 1 in each stitch across the neck area, make 5 stitches in the last stitch.

Finish off wool leaving a tail to attach the jacket to body.

Collar – In white

1. Chain 21, make 1 in the second chain from the hook and along (20)

2. In the first stitch make 3 stitches, make 1 in the rest of the row, in the last stitch make 3 stitches.

Finish off, leave a length of wool to attach to neck later.

Tie – In red

1. 8mr

2. Chain 8. Skip the first stitch and make 1 in the remaining stitches to form the tie.

Finish off, leaving a length of wool to attach to the neck later.

Shoes – In black – Make two

1. 8mr

2. (1, inc) x4 (12)

3-4. Make 1 in each (12)

5. Make 1 in the next 8 stitches, chain 1 turn your work. (8)

6-8. Repeat row 5.

Finish off, leave a length of wool.

Sew the heel together using s/s on each shoe.

Hands – In flesh – Make two

1. 6mr

2. (1, inc) (9)

3-8. Make 1 in each (9)

Finish off flesh colour.

Arms – In blue

Repeat for both arms.

75

Join at previous finish off point of flesh colour for hands.

1. Make 1 in each (9)
2. (1, inc) x4, 1 (13)
3. Make 1 in the next 12 stitches, (inc) x1 in the last stitch. (15)
4-12. Make 1 in each (15)
13. (dec) x7, make 1 in the remaining stitch.

Finish off, leaving a length of wool to attach to body later.

To make the poppy.

Using red wool.

In a magic circle, make 2 stitches and a slip stitch, make two stitches and a slip stitch, make 3 stitches and a slip stitch.

Finish off red wool.

Ears – In flesh - Make two

1. 6mr
2. (1, inc) (9)

Finish off, leaving a long tail to attach to head.

Hair – In deep orange.

1. 6mr
2. (inc) (12)
3. (1, inc) (18)
4. (2, inc) (24)
5. (3, inc) (30)
6. (4, inc) (36)
7. (5, inc) (42)
8-13. Make 1 in each (42)
14. Make 1 in the next 28, *chain 5 and make 1 in the second chain from the hook and 1 in the next 3 and slip stitch to the next*.

Repeat from * to * twice.

Continue making 1 in each stitch for the next 11 to complete round 14.

Finish off, leaving a length of wool to attach to head.

Construction.

*Sew hair to head, ensuring the three pieces are above the right eyebrow.

Using the wool, add eyebrows and sideburns.

*Add the ears under the hairline, in line with the nose.

*Sew the jacket to the shoulders and arms to the sides of the body.

*Lightly stuff the feet and sew to the legs.

*Insert a safety eye through the centre of the poppy and secure through the lapel of the jacket using the safety back.

Meghan

Meghan

Head – In flesh colour

1. 6mr

2. (inc) x6 (12)

3. (1, inc) x6 (18)

4. (2, inc) x6 (24)

5. (3, inc) x6 (30)

6. (4, inc) x6 (36)

7. (5, inc) x6 (42)

8. (6, inc) x6 (48)

9 – 12. Make 1 stitch in each (48)

13. Make 1 in the next 24 stitches, (P/B) x1, Make 1 in the remaining 23 stitches (48)

14 – 15. Make 1 in each stitch (48)

16. (6, dec) x6 (42)

17. (5, dec) x6 (36)

18. (4, dec) x6 (30)

19. (3, dec) x6 (24)

20. (2, dec) x6 (18)

21. (1, dec) x6 (12)

Insert eyes at row 11 with five stitches in-between and stuff the head.

22-23. Make 1 in each (12)

24.(inc, 1) x1, make 1 in the next 3, (inc) x1, make 1 in the remaining 6 stitches (14)

25. Make 1 in the next 4 stitches, (inc) x2, Make 1 in the next 6 stitches, (inc) x2 (18)

26. Make 1 in each stitch (18).

Finish off flesh colour.

Dress - In sage green

Joint green in the previous finish off point.

1. (6, inc) x1, make 1 in the next 2 stitches, (inc) x4, make 1 in the remaining 5 stitches (23)

2. Make 1 in the next 10 stitches, (inc,3, inc) x1, make 1 in the next 3 stitches, (3, inc, 2) (26)

3-4. Make 1 in each (26)

5. Make 1 in the next 11, (dec) x6, make 1 in the remaining 3 stitches (20)

6-7. Make 1 in each (20)

8. Make 1 in the next 7 stitches, (inc) x3, make 1 in the next 7 stitches, (inc) x3 (26)

9. (10, inc) x1, (11, inc) x1, make 1 in the remaining 3 stitches (28)

10-14. Make 1 in each (28)

15. Turn your work to face away from you and make 1 front post crochet around. (28)

16. Turn your work the correct way of working.

Make 1 in the next 5 stitches, count 14 stitches around and make a slip stitch to form the leg holes. Continue making another 1 in each for the next 14 and join to the first slip stitch, continue making 1 stitch in the next 7 to finish the round. (28)

Finish off wool and stuff the body.

Legs – In flesh colour

Repeat for each leg

1. Join at any point of row 14 and make 1 in each (14)

2. (4, dec) x2, make 1 in the last 2 remaining stitches (12)

3-5. Make 1in each (12)

Finish off and stuff the legs.

Skirt edging – In sage green.

Re-join the wool on row 13 and make 1 in each around for two rows. (28)

Finish off wool.

Shoes – In sage green - Make two.

1. 8mr
2. (1, inc) x4 (12)
3-5. Make 1 in each (12)
6. Make 1 in the next 8 stitches, chain 1 and turn your work (8)
7-8. Make 1 in each (8)

Finish off wool and slip stitch the heel together to form the shoes. Leave a length of wool to attach to the legs.

Hands – In flesh – Make two.

1. 6mr
2. (1, inc) x3 (9)
3-12. Make 1 in each (9)

Finish off wool.

Collar – In sage green.

1. Chain 27, make 1 in the second chain from the hook and along (26)
2-6 Make 1 in each (26)

Finish off your work, leave a length of wool to attach to body.

To make the poppy.

Using red wool.

In a magic circle, make 2 stitches and a slip stitch, make two stitches and a slip stitch, make 3 stitches and a slip stitch.

Finish off red wool.

Hair – In dark brown.

1. 6mr

2. (inc) x6 (12)

3. (1, inc) x6 (18)

4. (2, inc) x6 (24)

5. (3, inc) x6 (30)

6. (4, inc) x6 (36)

7. (5, inc) x6 (42)

8. (6, inc) x6 (48)

9-13. Make 1 in each (48)

14. Make 1 in the next 20 stitches, chain 25 and *make 3 in the second chain from the hook and 3 in each along the chain, slip stitch to the next stitch*. Make 1 more slip stitch and chain 25, repeat from * to *

Finish off and leave a length of wool to sew to head.

Additional hair piece – In dark brown – Make two.

Chain 21, make 3 in the second chain from the hook and 3 in each along the length of the chain.

Finish off, leaving a length of wool to attach to the head.

For hair bun – In dark brown.

1. 6mr

2. (inc) x6 (12)

3. (1, inc) x6 (18)

4. (2, inc) x6 (24)

5. (3, inc) x6 (30)

6. Make 1 in each (30)

7. (3, dec) x6 (24)

8. (2, dec) x6 (18)

Finish off and leave a length of wool to sew to the back of the head.

Ears – In flesh – Make two

1. 6mr, do not join.

Finish off and leave a length to attach to head.

Hat -In sage green

1. 6mr

2. (inc) x6 (12)

3. (1, inc) x6 (18)

4. (2, inc) x6 (24)

5. (2, dec) x6 (18)

6. (1, dec) x6 (12)

7. Chain 10, skip 1 stitch and slip stitch into the next, repeat * to * a total of six times.

Finish off and leave a length of wool to attach to the head.

Construction.

* Sew the hair to the head, using the brown wool add eyebrows.

Add the additional hair pieces around the hairline and the bun to the back of the head.

*Sew the ears to the side of the head, under the hairline, in line with the nose.

* Sew arms to the side of the body, in line with the top of the dress, add the collar over the arms and secure.

* Lightly stuff the feet and sew to the legs.

*Sew hat to the head.

*Place a safety eye through the centre of the poppy and secure to the collar using the safety back.

* Add accessories, i.e. earrings.

Printed in Great Britain
by Amazon